FRED

The Real Life Adventures

of a Little Girl with a Big Imagination

NATALIE BUSKE THOMAS

Copyright © 2016 Natalie Buske Thomas

All rights reserved.

ISBN: 9780966691948
ISBN-13: 978-0-9666919-4-8

DEDICATION

This book is dedicated to my husband Brent and my three children Cassandra, Nicholas, and Savannah.

AUTHOR'S WORKS

Grandpa Smiles
Dramatic Mom
Savannah's Inky Imagination
Nana Plays
10 Chapters series (Fender, Mol)
The Magic Camera
The Serena Wilcox Mysteries (Gene Play, Virtual Memories, Camp Conviction, Angels Mark, Covert Coffee, Bluebird Flown, Project Scarecrow, Ruby Red, Future Beyond, Project Willow, Downward Spiral, Shed Secrets)
Faith According to You
Nice Authors Finish Last
We are the Angels that He Sends
Thriving in a Hateful World
Ramen Noodles and Hot Dogs
The Miracle Dulcimer

Watch Natalie paint the illustrations from this book!

www.NataliesArtandBooks.com

SOMETHING YOU NEED TO KNOW

Hi, my name is Fred. Well, not really. I was given the name Natalie Marie at birth. My father said that when I was three years old I suddenly announced that from now on my name was Fred. I forgot all about this, but my father didn't. He called me Fred from that day onward.

This book is the story of me, Natalie—otherwise known as Fred.

P.S. When you're done reading the story, don't forget to watch me paint the pictures! www.NataliesArtandBooks.com

Fred had a big imagination. She didn't know what this meant exactly. It was something that people told her when they were surprised by Fred's ideas. Sometimes people acted like her ideas were a good surprise, but mostly, people narrowed their eyes and scrunched up their noses when they talked about her big imagination.

Fred wondered how it was possible NOT to have an imagination. What did people with no imagination dream about at night? Maybe they dreamt about sleeping.

People without an imagination probably said the same things every day. They probably *did* the same things every day. Every day was probably exactly the same as the one before it.

Fred noticed that her art teacher, Mrs. S, said the same things every day. That meant that she probably did the same things every day. And she probably had dreams about sleeping!

Fred was convinced that having a big imagination wasn't a bad thing, even though sometimes people made it sound like it was.

Mrs. S was one of those people.

Mrs. S didn't like Fred's big imagination. She held up Fred's paper and said, "There's no special way you have to do it, but don't do it like Natalie."

Mrs. S didn't know that Natalie was secretly Fred. If she had known, maybe then she would have also known that Fred would never copy the teacher's example! Why would Fred copy someone else's ideas when she had plenty of her own?

Every art class began and ended the same way. Fred really did try to make Mrs. S happy, but somehow her imagination always got the best of her. It was too hard to resist drawing her own pictures on the paper.

Soon Fred would be so caught up in her own ideas that she would hardly notice anything going on around her. She'd almost forget that she was in school. She definitely forgot the example that Mrs. S had shown her.

No matter how good Fred's intentions had been at the beginning of class, by the end of it Fred would be lost in her own world. And once again, Mrs. S would hold up Fred's art as an example of what NOT to do.

She always said the same thing, in the exact same way, while using the same scratchy voice. "There's no special way you have to do it, but don't do it like Natalie."

Fred looked forward to summer time, when there was no school and she could play with her cousins at Grandma and Grandpa's. Unfortunately, it was a long drive from Fred's house in Indiana to her grandparents' house in upstate New York. Worst of all, she had to sit next to her little brother for twelve hours straight.

Fred drew an invisible line between their seats. Jeffrey always ignored the line completely as if it wasn't even there! Sometimes they played Slug Bug. The rules were simple. Any time they saw a Volkswagen Beetle, the first to shout "Punch buggy, no return!" would punch their sibling in the shoulder. They weren't supposed to make it hurt, but after too many hours of invisible lines being crossed, Fred broke the rules.

Hour after hour they drove. They drove all through the night! Fred and Jeffrey always fell asleep eventually. The car was quiet then. Finally, sometimes before the sun was up, they'd arrive at Grandma and Grandpa's familiar blue house on the hill.

But Fred didn't always stay at Grandma and Grandpa's. She couldn't resist a game of Goose Tag. It was way scarier than playing Slug Bug with Jeffrey, who stayed behind with the little kids when Fred went with her cousins next door.

The rules of Goose Tag were simple. The last kid to jump on the neighbor's porch got bit on the you-know-where. Too bad Natalie was the smallest and slowest. And the geese didn't know that she was secretly Fred! In fact, no one noticed that Natalie was Fred. If they had, maybe her cousins—and those horrible neighbor kids—wouldn't have goaded her into playing endless rounds of Goose Tag!

Sometimes Fred's parents went to Grandma and Grandpa's house for Christmas. The weather was always bad. It snowed a lot in New York. But Fred was never worried. Snow was fun! Someone always had a sled Fred could borrow, and Grandma always had a carrot handy for Fred's snowman.

Of course, after the house was full of relatives things got kind of crazy. Grandma didn't want to be pestered about such things as carrots for a snowman's nose then. Fred had to get all of her favors out of the way before the house started filling up. After that, Fred was stuck at the kiddie table for the holiday dinner hour. After dinner she was expected to play with her cousins, whether she wanted to or not.

If the grownups were tired of seeing the kids hanging around, they'd tell them all to play outside. If it was cold, they'd say, "Then bundle up." There was no use in talking back. When the grownups were all together they were stronger than when they were on their own. Sometimes three or four of the mothers would say the same thing at the same time!

It was on one of those chilly winter days when Fred and her cousins were huddled together on Grandpa's front porch. Fred sat by the steps, next to an icy black metal post. One of her cousins said, "I dare you to put your tongue on it." Fred wasn't chicken—she proved it by touching her tongue to the post. Fred's tongue stuck fast! She tried to wriggle free, but it hurt too much.

Her cousins raced to the door, flung it open, and burst inside the warm kitchen where everyone was chatting and drinking tea. They rushed to be the first to tell the grownups what had happened. "Natalie got her tongue stuck to the pole!" After pouring warm water over Fred's tongue she was free from the post. The grownups were shocked that she would do something so stupid. Well, Natalie was always sensible. But they should have known that Fred could never resist a dare!

Fred also couldn't resist adventure, even when Natalie knew better. Fred let her friend Kathy talk her into riding a big bicycle for the first time—a bicycle that could shift gears. Fred's feet could barely touch the pedals.

Kathy insisted that she rode a big bicycle all the time and that her favorite place to ride was on a nearly-hidden narrow gravel road that dropped off sharply into a steep descent that seemed to go on forever. Fred couldn't even see the bottom. How far did it go?

Fred didn't know that Kathy was fibbing. She had never been on a big bicycle either. And she had most certainly never ridden down the treacherous hill! Fred would learn all of this from Kathy's parents later, but by then it would be too late. Kathy had already started down the hill. Fred followed her.

Seconds into the ride the hill was too much for Kathy. She crashed the bicycle and let out an ear-piercing shriek. When she saw that her knee was sliced open and blood was gushing out, Kathy screamed continuously. Fred tried to block out the screams. She had to focus! She too was fast losing control over her bicycle.

Fred didn't know how to make the bicycle stop. She was going much too fast. Dust whirled as her wheels hit the gravel. The bicycle had taken on a life of its own. Fred had long stopped pedaling. She tried to hold steady while the tires skidded and skipped over the loose gravel. Fred could feel the gravel scattering under her wheels. The faster the bicycle went, the slipperier the gravel became.

Suddenly Fred was airborne. In that smallest of seconds Fred knew that she was about to get hurt. She hit the ground with a painful thud around the same time that the bicycle landed without her on it.

Natalie's mother looked at the bloody scrapes on her head, elbow, and knee. She said, "What made you think that you could do a thing like that?"

Natalie's father drove down the big hill to see what all the fuss was about. There wasn't enough traction under his car's tires and the hill was much too steep. They got to the bottom safely, but it wasn't easy. Natalie's father was flabbergasted! "What part of this seemed like a good idea?"

Fred didn't know how to explain that ALL exciting ideas seem good at the start. She didn't plan to fall off the bike. Kathy had told her that she had ridden down that hill all the time. How was she to know that Kathy had been fibbing? And besides, had her father forgotten that she was Fred?

Fred's adventures led her to all kinds of places. She loved to explore creek beds in search of minnows, but she had to watch out for broken glass. People littered with bottles and other trash. Fred thought of it as an obstacle course, like the game of Hot Lava that she played with Jeffrey.

The rules for Hot Lava were simple: hop from one stepping stone to another, then keep going until all players were bored with the game or had fallen too many times into the "hot lava", otherwise known as the floor. The best stepping stones were the couch cushions that she and Jeffrey scattered on the living room carpet. They leapt from cushion to cushion, from blanket to blanket, and from pillow to pillow.

Except that Fred was never really in danger when playing Hot Lava. The broken glass at the creek bed was real. Fred was extra careful during her real life adventures. She almost fell, but she never did. She was always careful.

Fred's adventures led her up trees and on secret missions. One of the boys next door was a spy but he didn't know it. It was up to Fred and Jeffrey to stop him! Fred was stealth. She had a lot of patience and she could outlast anyone. She watched quietly, waiting for the exact moment when the spy was standing directly under her tree. That was when she struck! She released pine cones onto the spy's head.

The spy spun around, looking for his attacker. Seeing no one, he was confused. He looked a little frightened. He ran away. Mission complete!

Fred could have been a spy forever, but she eventually became bored with being a spy. Besides, Jeffrey couldn't be trusted not to blow their cover. Jeffrey always giggled when the spy ran away.

One lazy summer day, Fred was bored. She was so bored that she lay on her back with her toes high above her head. She balanced a rock between her feet. She held the rock with her toes and passed it from one foot to the other.

Suddenly the rock slipped! Like Fred's pine cone in a tree, the rock was in exactly the right position to drop onto Fred's face below. The rock was a direct hit to her mouth, giving her a bloody and quickly-swelling fat lip.

Fred's mother said, "Why did you do that?"

Fred's father said, "What part of this seemed like a good idea?"

Fred didn't know how to explain that good ideas were the problem. Sometimes her head was noisy with good ideas! Her brain was like the abstract art that Fred had learned about in school, the kind of paintings that had no pictures on them.

If Fred's father could see inside her brain he'd see bold colors that moved and swirled. Fred imagined what this art would look like. It would have plenty of yellow and green like the tree forest where she and Jeffrey pretended to be spies. It would have blue in it like the ocean. There was no ocean in Indiana or New York, but she was going to live by the sea one day. She just knew it.

Her art would have the colors of a rainbow—in the rain itself! There would have to be red. Red was Fred's favorite color. She needed more yellow and she could mix it with red to make orange. Those were the colors of the sun, and she loved sunny rainy days.

Fred decided that her brain was a rainbow-y rainy day while the sun was shining, AND she'd add a stretch of white puffy clouds too, the kind of clouds that are thin, wispy, and alone in the sky.

Purples, browns, and more of all of the other colors were like a field of flowers. Fred would add those too. Yes, Fred's brain was full of color and good ideas. It's no wonder that rocks fell on her face sometimes.

Fred knew that her parents were right. She had better things to do than balancing a rock on her feet. Fred decided to write a play. She cast Jeffrey and the boys next door to act in it. She made costumes and set the date for when they would do the show. Next, she made flyers. She and her acting troupe delivered the flyers to the neighbors.

The patio became a stage. They set chairs up in the backyard and waited for the neighbors to arrive. They came! When everyone was in the audience the show began.

Fred was now a playwright, a theater director, and an actress. Why there was nothing that she couldn't do!

Soon summer turned into fall and it was time for another school year. As usual, Fred brought home amazingly high assessment test scores, with a note to her parents that read, "Natalie is not achieving at her full potential."

Fred's father said, "I'm disappointed in you. I know you can do better."

Fred's mother said, as if Fred wasn't even in the room, "She's daydreaming in class."

Fred didn't know how to explain that her classes were so boring that the only way she could survive them was to draw while the teacher was talking. Sometimes she drew pictures of storybook animals from her future book series, for when she would become a famous author. Sometimes she drew hearts and doodles. Other times, when she was particularly sneaky, she drew cartoons of her teachers. Usually she only did this when her teachers deserved it by being extra boring.

Fred didn't always underachieve. She did well in her creative writing class – all A's! She loved music and she was an excellent dancer. She lit up the stage in her recitals, winning enough dance trophies to start a collection. Fred even won the school magazine's short story contest for her strange tale about aliens who stole human children.

In Fred's mind she was a success!

The years flew by. Fred graduated from high school with her friends. Soon she would be off to college!

Natalie, the girl secretly named Fred, was growing up.

College wasn't as much fun as Fred thought that it would be. The classes were long and boring. Sometimes she imagined that the clock was ticking backwards instead of forwards. And worst of all, her art class felt no better than the one she took when she was in elementary school.

Fred tried to make her college professor happy, but somehow she never did the assignments the way that he expected her to do them. He held up her paper as an example of what NOT to do. Then, while the entire class was still listening and watching, he told Natalie that she would never be an artist.

That was the last straw! Natalie quit taking art classes. What was the use if she would never be an artist? She studied business and German instead. It was time to be practical.

Natalie's parents had been right. She spent too much time daydreaming. Maybe if she stopped doodling in class she'd get better grades. In fact, Natalie decided to stop doing art even when she wasn't in school. What was the point? She didn't even like it anymore anyway.

Natalie struggled through college. She couldn't make straight A's, not even when she gave up art and tried her best to focus. She wished she had been born a different person. Maybe then she could be someone important, like a doctor or a scientist.

Don't worry, Natalie didn't stay practical for long because Fred was not a quitter! Her big imagination always got the best of her. When she saw an advertisement for a talent show she couldn't resist entering it.

She asked a favor from a friend. Her friend sat on the stage, posing for a picture. Fred drew the girl's face fast, on a big easel—live during the show! The judges were mightily impressed. And she won! A short while after that she entered an arts festival. She drew cartoons for $2 each. Her pockets were soon full of dollars!

Years passed. Fred got married, moved far away from home, and had three children. Even though she was grown up now, she still got hurt. Sometimes the hurt was on the outside, like when she fell off the big bicycle on the steep hill. Most of the time, the hurt was on the inside, like when her art teachers told her that she wasn't good enough.

But she never ever gave up! When one dream ended, she dreamt up another. One day she decided that it was her dream to paint in Ireland. She sold almost everything that she had and flew across the big ocean with her husband and three children. For five months she lived on that beautiful green island near the sea.

She saw a dolphin in the wild named Fungie. She painted pictures, like she said that she would. Then, just like that, she flew back home again. Her biggest dream had come true! From then on, Natalie was no longer *secretly* Fred, but *always* Fred.

Are you surprised that Natalie became a playwright, an actress, a theater director, a teacher, an author, and… an ARTIST? Now gallery walls hold Natalie's art for the whole world to see. It turns out that there *is* a special way to do it after all. And she's done it!

Never listen to people who tell you that you aren't good enough.

Always do what you were born to do—
like Fred does.

ABOUT THE AUTHOR

Natalie Buske Thomas is the author of over twenty-five books and an oil painter with art in galleries and on tour. Natalie has lived in New York, Indiana, Germany, Minnesota, Wisconsin, and Ireland. Her dream of writing and painting in Ireland came true. She even saw a dolphin in the wild, up close and personal!

Natalie loves people who are full of passion and imagination. She likes playing the drums, going on adventures with her family, watching funny shows on TV, taking pictures, eating, and singing. Her favorite color is red. She loves cake and cookies. Her favorite cookies are sugar, peanut butter, oatmeal chocolate chip, half-moon, and her own secret recipe—Nat's Chocolate Chip Cookies.

www.ingramcontent.com/pod-product-compliance
Lightning Source LLC
Chambersburg PA
CBHW042014090426
42811CB00015B/1644